Pocket Sundial

Pocket Sundial

LISA ZEIDNER

The University of Wisconsin Press

The University of Wisconsin Press
1930 Monroe Street, 3rd floor
Madison, Wisconsin 53711-2059
uwpress.wisc.edu

3 Henrietta Street
London WC2E 8LU, England
eurospanbookstore.com

Printed in the United States of America

Library of Congress Cataloging-in-Publication Data
Zeidner, Lisa.
    Pocket sundial.
    (The Brittingham prize in poetry)
    I. Title.   II. Title: Pocket sun dial.   III. Series.
PS3576.E37P6   1988   811'.54   88-40196
ISBN 0-299-11920-3
ISBN 0-299-11924-6 (pbk.)

ISBN-13: 978-0-299-11924-9 (pbk: alk. paper)

FOR JOHN LAFONT

Not until the sixteenth century could sundials be marked with the true hours. When this "science of dialing" was developed, it became fashionable to carry a pocket sundial. But by then the clock and the watch existed and were more convenient and useful in every way.

—Daniel J. Boorstin, *The Discoverers*

Contents

Acknowledgments

Grateful acknowledgment is made to the editors of the following magazines in which these poems first appeared:

Boulevard: "Bat and Skyscraper" and "The Collector's Fire"

Epoch: "Saturday Morning Cartoons"

Gulf Coast: "Happiness"

The Mississippi Review: "Baltimore Avenue," "Dementia Collander," "Dying in Your Dreams," "Gypsy Moths," "Lesson," "Needlepoint Guernica," and "Sweeping"

The New Republic: "Child's Moon"

The Painted Bride Quarterly: "The Mesopotamian Tool Room"

Poetry: "A Bomb," "Safety in Numbers," and "What Really Happens When the Plane Goes Down"

Raccoon: "Woman, 78, Caught Shoplifting"

Shenandoah: "Decisions, Decisions," copyright © 1987 by Washington and Lee University, reprinted from *Shenandoah*: The Washington and Lee University Review

Three Rivers Poetry Journal: "Transvestite" and "Pothole," copyright © 1987 by Three Rivers Press

West Branch: "Bach's Other Sixteen Children"

One

A Bomb

Afterwards, we'll all remember
having seen it coming.
A trick of mind, like déjà vu:
how sometimes, while being witty
over drinks, with dishes
in the sink or hand on the door
of a cabinet wherein lie
the last cashews dusted with salt
at the bottom of a jar
when you're not even hungry,
the mind summons a picture of a place
shocking in its specificity—

a certain block, a house belonging
to no one you knew in the old
neighborhood, or turning a corner
in a city you visited once
on business years ago
and haven't thought about since.
So hard to accept
irrelevance, irregularity.
Much easier to think the picture means
to tell you something, warn you,
but of what? Of where you'll die?
Maybe, since all your death will be—

all anybody's—is that shudder
like a random memory, not a burglar
at the back door but something
on the house's own quirky,
undecipherable Richter Scale,
so minor you must have imagined it.

Pothole

Cars are the sheep
urban insomniacs count.
Traffic stripes the bedroom
like light through Venetian blinds,
so as your gondola is oared towards sleep

you pass beneath
storeys, a wall of noise—
the wall decaying, that's inevitable,
but inevitability is grand;
decay is an urban phenomenon

so perennial it's almost pastoral,
and look how winter is defied
by the geranium or other
red, living thing in
that window, below

the window where
the dark woman leans
out, mistaking your sleep
for a gondola bearing her lover
who will, of course, bear flowers—

but this was all before the pothole.
With this new pothole the noise
is rerouted to your pillow:
first the thump, *bachow*
like a Chinese sneeze,

then the Batman *clatarata*
of the hubcaps (usually one per
car, but drunkards taking the curve
at seventy per—there's justice here—
sometimes lose two or three)

4

hurling curbward like the frisbees
that pass for flying saucers
in late night movies.
What a racket!
Your sleep,

at this rate,
will never get deeper
than a pothole; your mind is
ungainly and dry as a hippopotamus
bathing in a puddle, and rest is

somewhere you can
no more get from here
than a prisoner can dig
a tunnel to—Venice would do.
You won't need to know the language;

you'll manage *pasta*,
amore, peel bills from your pocket
like Zeus flicking thunderbolts
until you're spent, so little left
you can hide in tire treads

to slip small and free through
pothole and street, and you
thought you'd never arrive!
But you did, not just in
Italy but ancient

Rome, then
even deeper back,
so by morning, you think
the noisy trash men are from
distant times, oaring a barge up the Nile.

Baltimore Avenue

The North wind blows the trash onto our lawn.
The South wind blows it off. Or maybe
it's an East wind, and a West—
I am no specialist. In any case
there is always flotsam and
jetsam on our lawn. In certain frames
of mind the ebb and flow of trash
can seem quite natural, the corn
chip bag, the twisted pull-top tab,
the scrap of stock market page in a bottle
of Night Express like a cryptic message from
the deep: *Invest!* In the distance,
the foghorn of a double-parked car impatient
to set sail, trailing a broken muffler
like the howl of a mutineer
about to be devoured by sharks.

Transvestite

How easy to tell it's a man,
though the gestures are feminine.
Popeye jawline and hands
scaled too large—coltish,
as if he simply hasn't finished
growing into his gender—clash
with red heels and wafty dress.

The overkill of sexual semaphore
is a dead giveaway,
as the nouveau riche in their fur,
jewels and chauffeured limousines
bespeak insecurity, not luxury,
but then whores also dress whorishly,
hence the doubletake:

maybe just a squarish, gaudy woman?
No. Behind him in line
for tickets at the train station,
I smell something indescribably male
that turns the perfume petrochemical.
The smell is animal, hormonal,
more real and subtle than the way

hairy legs, hairy chests and baritones
leak through to blow the drag cover
of wolves in sheep's clothing
in old movies like "Some Like It Hot."
To think the whole masquerade
only serves to attract other men—why not,
in this day and age, simply be gay?

Because nothing is simple, especially sex,
though maybe not for most quite this complex:
a comedy of errors in which a boy actor
dresses up as a girl who dresses up as a boy,
except at the end of the play
order is restored, "and so to bed"
with the destined mate,

whereas in real life all the world's a stage
or a train station—entrances, exits,
nothing permanent except the state of flux,
the lockers monopolized
by the homeless who enjoy here
if not camouflage, at least a little peace.
The travelers keep their distance,

stare obliquely, as they do at the transvestite.
Staring myself, I think of dead opossums
on the highway, of civilization's savagery,
wishing the poor guy could be
in a jungle somewhere, tall
and fit, naked except for a single,
simple loincloth.

Safety in Numbers

Highway center lanes, movie center seats
are popular not only
because the golden mean is cozy
as a child holding hands
with both parents, but because—

that old paradox—they're popular:
nothing succeeds like success.
Three men in a tub, thirty men
in a phone booth, all you can eat,
presents heaped under the tree:

more is usually merrier;
though they say clichés get that way
by being fresh originally,
the first cause is more often than not
the response and not the stimulus.

Gape at blank sky
until you get a following
for a tried-and-true demonstration
of how the emperor went naked
and of the Third Reich.

By the law of averages,
bounty must entail conformity.
We're all the smartest kid in the class,
a party of one, a bandwagon
of first kids on the block.

It's mandatory, for instance,
to mistrust a generalization,
"blonds have more fun" being, after all,
an Aryan sentiment, even supported
by (doubtless rigged) statistics.

Our unilateral insistence
on going against the grain
is glorified sibling rivalry: our heroes
identically outfit hordes of Nazis
and Turks with one-track minds

to fulfill our fantasy
of the blessedness of only children
(how much attention Jesus got!),
a union of Lone Rangers who know
that all beds are Procrustean,

all designer dresses
have other women in them.
Democracy is also a tyranny.
It cancels, equalizes controversy.
"Very nice, dear," it says

to all its children
like an indulgent mother who lives
in a shoe and hangs everyone's
art on the refrigerator.
If, as Blake says,

"to generalize is to be an idiot,"
then that generalization is idiotic
(let Blake eat raw pork), as is
the contention that it's no better
to rob Ma Bell than to rob

a Mom-and-Pop store,
no less heinous to kill one man
than to kill a million—
to begin, it takes more bullets.
The point is, we're still counting.

We wouldn't hurt a fly and we pick up
the tab, but we keep tabs
on our tolerance, our generosity.
The Taoists, who advise us
to leap into the infinite

and make it our home, must realize
that once the boundless is a home
you can't vacation there;
the boundless then has doors, a mortgage,
an acreage larger or smaller

than the Jones's; though a house
isn't always a home and though you can't
please all the people all the time,
the odds are good
that the boundless is best visited.

The rest of the time, ceilings not only
keep down the heating bill
but provide a satisfying known variable
against which to assess
the real mysteries, like love or cancer.

There's safety, in short, not only
in numbers, but in the numbers of those
who oppose the safety of numbers
and even in the ranks of devil's advocate—
each way, you're in good company.

Child's Moon

Eyes don't grow.
That's why a baby's eyes look big.
While the length of the adult body
buried like a time bomb
in the soft bones
pushes out, the eyes,
like scars, remain the same.

The eggs, I hear, are in there
too, from day one.
As women age so do their eggs.
Some are shrivelled and tough
as elephant skin; sadly,
those eggs travel their routes
like the ghosts of retired mailmen

while in the brain—
that dead-letter office—everything
that ever happened to you
remains, each tune you hummed,
each lunch, fact, caress.
A stroke or seizure can call forth
a particular summer dusk.

In the future, we may
be able to eradicate bad memories
with electrical prods precisely applied
to the temporal lobes, more efficient
than psychoanalysis, more amazing
than men on the moon.
How slowly they planted colorless flags

in earth, stone, or dust—I can't remember
now, it was so long ago we watched them
then picnicked in our own back yard.
We were allowed to stay up
until the print on our pajamas
turned sooty and vibrated
in half-light, like the moon.

In lightyears we were put to bed.
Our parents waved and waved,
distant as the moon men
or as we are now, as adults,
from our own insides,
from each of our secret,
whisper-jet travel towards death.

Sweeping

Beethoven, bored,
alone at home, hefts
himself from the piano bench
and, with a broom, begins
to push dust into a dustpan.

I like to imagine
the Ode to Joy
came to him while sweeping.
Sick of invention, he bent
and brushed, the dust pretty

as gold in the pan
though hardly an arpeggio
for Ludwig, happily, was deaf.
We resent mere genius
but blind painters,

limping cowboys and deaf
composers are underdogs
who earn their triumphs.
O friends, not these sounds!
What? Beethoven bends his head

to the dustpan, as if
to hear the ocean there,
and hears a line from Schiller,
from a poem he loves which for
a decade has been brain-dust,

a mote but mute,
and now a note, floating
then—*Freude!*—anchored
to another note.
Dust was his inspiration.

He almost choked from joy.
Joy fell like an apple
on his head as it did
when sweeping, bored,
I thought of him.

Bach's Other Sixteen Children

Wilhelm Friedemann, the oldest son,
was his father's favorite
but had a bad temper and lived
a hermit's life, died poor at 74.
Carl Phillip Emmanuel, the second son,
befriended the Crown Prince Frederick
of Frankfort and though slight
of build, often accused of triviality,
became more famous than his father
after his essay "On the True Art
of Playing Keyboard Instruments."

If C.P.E. achieved the marriage
of *Empfindsamkeit* (sentimentality)
with the Style Galant, then Kapellmeister
J.C.F. (Johann Cristoph Friederich)
was the only one to have a musical child
himself—Wilhelm Friedrich Ernst lived to 81.
Johann Christian married an Italian, wrote opera.
As for the other sixteen children
of Anna Magdalena, the Princely Singer
and Bach's second wife (the first,
Maria Barbara, died after a year),

were they proud to be Bachs? Jealous?
Did they all take turns washing
the dishes, or just the girls?
Did their mother love them equally?
It must have been a noisy house
with all those instruments and pregnancies;
with all those pregnancies it must have been
a loving place as well. J.S., home
from work, pats the children on the head
one by one (all of them were called,
for some reason, by their middle names)

then in the kitchen finds his wife,
a hand on her swollen belly
and a whisper the children can't overhear:
> *Do not demand glances*
> *of my love from me,*
> *envy's tangled traps*
> *are turned toward us.*
> *You must lock your breast,*
> *contain your inclination.*
> *The desire which we enjoy*
> *must remain a secret.*

The Collector's Fire

Losing music hurt the most.
He had every composer's every piece
in almost every performance,
often in multiple copies in case of—
not fire but scratches, dust,
all matter's gravitation to decay.
Most albums he would never
have listened to anyway,
but the best and worst rarities
are the 1% he could never replace.

For the other 99%
he could call Tower Records and say
"Send me one of everything,"
but he still wouldn't have
what he most loved,
and it would be obscene
as trying to duplicate
in a fast-motion day
a lifetime's sexual experience,
a lifetime's longing and release.

What died with the records is time
because music was his bodily clock
and fire has no rhythm.
Fire is impossible to score.
It happens in a glacial silence
as if timber died when timbre did
though the words aren't twins,
not even distant relatives:
timber is a building or building material
in Middle English, hence the tree felled

and falling loudly in the Old West,
while timbre is a drum or bell
struck in Old French and heard
in *tympanum,* the middle ear—but enough.
The dictionary burned too.
This is the kind of thing
the collector liked to do
before the fire, before the fire:
alone with music in the library,
the dictionary warm as a lapped cat,

the magnifying glass shedding light
on one root of one word in a language
denser than cat hair,
timber and timbre mirroring
the way words can be neighbors
yet worlds apart,
like *ante* and *anti,* Latin and Greek,
before the fire and against it.
You need leisure to care about language.
Without time—and fire kills time—

there is no leisure, just time
to shout *Fire!* and run.
"Luckily," the newspaper said—
how often the collector has wanted to burn
the paper, to make a bonfire
(which is not a good fire,
bon as in *bonbon* or *bon mot,*
but *banfyre,* a place for burning bones)—
"the collector was not at home
at the time of the fire."

In the time it takes to say
at the time, the fire ate
antiques and antique rugs,
records, books, paintings—
"while," the paper added,
"the multimillionaire was abroad,
augmenting his collection."
Ate: how easy to personify fire.
Fire is gluttonous, like the collector.
The newspapers ate it up.

You can't take it with you, so why bother?
Fire is a great equalizer, since
like a goat or shark it eats everything,
the slapdash farmer's chair
and the museum-quality Shaker
licked identically by flames.
Sometimes he wishes he *had* died
though a house is not a ship
you're expected to go down with.
The hero escapes, having rescued

whatever he can't live without.
The collector saw on TV once
a grinning man in a bathrobe
containing a noisy bird
tailfeathers of which had been charred
to resemble a quill pen dipped in ink,
but generally TV shuns the comic fire.
TV firemen like best to carry out
rescued children, limp Pietàs in Dr. Dentons.

Life itself is what's supposed to count,
not the shirt on your back.
God, the television fires!
One minute of tragedy like a commercial,
artificial as the moment of silence
and as useless a prophylactic,
though the point is let us pause now
and be glad it happened to someone else,
the superstition being that each fire
reduces the odds of another—

like lightning or chicken pox
we assume one per customer.
In his hotel room now
the collector hits the remote control
which obedient as a butler
kills the evening news
when it moves to the daily two-alarmers,
though he watched and cried
when a famous athlete lost his house to fire.
The athlete, too, had records, rugs.

Like the collector, an investment banker,
what the athlete did depended on timing,
on seconds split precise
as melons karate-chopped in half
by a Japanese chef, so he would similarly hate
ten seconds demolishing a rug
that took ten years to make, each loop
hand-stitched, in silk, by slaves.
The insurance covered everything
except the irreplaceable,

which was everything.
To "start afresh" would be
to plant saplings in Levittown.
But why, one reporter asked—
the only one he spoke to, a mistake
though she was young, and pretty—
why not buy another mansion,
with acreage and huge old elms?
That would be, he said, rebuilding the pyramids
once the mummies were stolen.

But why not at least stay at a good hotel?
He could not explain the room
at the Holiday Inn with its bed, chair, desk,
its bible and phone book, its harvest theme
in the sickliest orange, fire orange.
He could not make love to the journalist
though he tried, knew
he was eligible as bachelors go,
knew the best object is a human object,
one that can love back.

She still calls: "You ought to get out,"
the collector unable to concentrate
for the odd pizzicato of *out* and *ought,*
the *G-H* all the difference
between being free and knowing you should be.
Beside the TV, the eight-foot Aphrodite
he bought on that last trip
is still swaddled in white.
At first he couldn't bear to see her,
then he began to like the way she looked

veiled and roped—safe, free
as the records were in the old days
from dust, sunlight, the grit of fingers.
Sometimes, late, when the mummy
is illuminated by street lamps
through the prison blinds, he swears he can hear
her shifting in the amnion of cloth,
can see the voluptuousness of the marble flesh
and beneath that, cool
and white, her skeleton.

What Really Happens When the Plane Goes Down

There isn't time
for change of heart, forgive and forget
or any resolution of plot
such as movies use
to chart disaster like a dance step.

Because you kissed someone
once extra at the door
you get to the corner in time
to watch the bus, sharp
as a shark's fin,

escaping you.
Like your life, the plane
is a kite in a tree—too light,
and not strong enough. Fluff.
There is only time

for a spasm of regret:
if you'd only known
you'd miss the bus,
you would have made the kiss
more memorable.

Dementia Colander

The disease from which the King suffered
is named for its discoverer,
Rainer Colanderi—the *i* slipped overboard
in his translation to our island,
which welcomed his research
before beheading him
in the Fuchsia Siege.

The great phrenologist himself,
a German-Italian ladies' man
with a tortoiseshell monocle
and impeccable cuticles,
suffered from the malady,
and in fact there is speculation
that his classic monograph,

"A Pitiful Affliction of Kings"
(known for its thumbnail sketch
of Lucy H., with her shiver and cleavage)
was inspired by an active spell
of the disease, for with Dementia C.
the disease is the cure, and vice versa.
The Queen knew all along.

During the charmed interlude
when hurricanes were minor,
as were plague and crusade, beside the joy
of being courted by the heir-apparent,
Queen Deirdre (then ten, soon to be pregnant
with her first and only son)
was in the royal garden

in the lap of her cousin
when he leapt up, jettisoning her
on her coccyx, and scrambled to one rose
on one of the thousand bushes.
Naturally Didi (as she was then known
to family) assumed that a rose
was forthcoming for her,

but Otis the Transfixed
(the nickname would stick) had squatted
to examine for hours
a rose not distinguished
by color, shape, size, or smell
and would not be torn away
by the future queen's endearments,

invitation to play phrenologist,
bared bodice, or, later, by his mother,
the present king his father, or his fool.
Ten soldiers had to carry him
passively resisting with "his doublet
all unbraced, his stockings
down-gyvèd to his ankles"

(this from Didi's diary, our best source
on the King and the court as well as
the inspiration for "Hamlet"—
it has been suggested, in fact,
that the prince's delay was not
cowardice, not an Oedipus Complex
but Dementia Colander)

to dinner, where he stared
at the apple in the suckling pig's mouth.
Pig devoured, carcass removed,
he stared at air,
and would not move for days.
A bedpan was brought,
a hole cut in his pantaloons

while the soldiers held him aloft
by the armpits, embarrassing everyone
concerned, especially Didi,
who was forced to marry him
post-haste under the theory
that what he needed was a good
lay—a theory that, it appears,

was correct at least temporarily
in the case of knock-kneed
and gangly, then fifteen-year-old Otis,
who abandoned his trance five days hence
cheerful, hungry, yawning,
oblivious to the fact
that five doctors had already thrown up

their hands and been executed.
The wedding was held in two months,
barely long enough to produce
the ceremony's velvet, ermine, and jewels.
The public, needless to say,
was not informed of Otis' condition
and those who had witnessed

his behavior at dinner
and thereafter were sworn
to secrecy, then executed, so only
the Queen knew of Otis' weakness,
the erstwhile king and queen
having perished together
in the "hunting accident"

commonly attributed to Joel the Good,
although Joel's accusers have never
provided a satisfactory motive
since Joel was already in office
and wisely refused promotions
in a regime that was,
like Dementia Colander itself,

fitful at best,
if less fitful than most,
for Otis was a family man.
Queen Deirdre assumed it was the death
of their son two years later
which provoked the King to stare
for days at the infant's tiny hands

permanently pressed into prayer.
Such a wake did not injure
public relations; Otis' image
as a thoughtful king, a king with heart,
impressed even the Queen, who hoped
she had been overhasty
in condemning her husband's sanity.

"He is transfixed only by grief,"
she told her diary; "who knows
what saddened him in the garden?"
Both science and conventional wisdom
corroborated her conviction
that neurasthenia and sensitivity
were twins; madness was common

as the cold among royalty,
a sign of good breeding.
As George the Third would apologize
when he interrupted ceremonies
to play the eight tunes he knew
for miniature mechanical organ
or to mourn his own death,

"I am nervous. I am not ill,
but I am nervous."
As long as Otis wore the diaper-like sling
the Queen had designed for him
after the wake incident—
not noticeable, or even uncomfortable,
given the bulk of garments currently

fashionable, though since Otis
was ignorant of his condition
Deirdre coaxed him to wear
the fur and silk belt
recently auctioned to a sheik
by inventing a sexual fetishism
for which she is unjustly canonized—

his trances passed for concentration.
If the King chose to spend a week
on his knees in the pantry
staring down a cornered mouse
that was his right, especially
if pity for the mouse helped him make
the most popular decision of his reign:

the removal of troops
placed in distant Latvia
by his bloodthirsty father.
Otis' trances were always followed
by significant decisions of state.
In this Dementia C. differs
from catatonia, Parkinson's, autism

and the other conditions
for which it is often misdiagnosed:
the spells do not leak through
to the rest of the victim's days
except as clarity; if anything
the illness is refreshing.
The accidental metaphor of the colander

misled the scientists after Colanderi
to portray the brain as a massive rock
in a colander which is the skull.
Also in the colander are flowerlets
from a head of broccoli—the ideas
which the victim tries to flush
through the colander into his mouth

as speech, or into his limbs
as movement (for even stabbing a pea
with a fork is an idea,
loosely translated).
Usually there is no problem:
the colander is not airtight
and like ideas, broccoli is malleable.

But the rock shifts or gets stuck,
the holes in the colander are clogged
and *voilà!* Otis is transfixed.
Like Plato, Freud would warn against
the "masquerading" of metaphors that are
"literature instead of science":
the word *sub* (not *un*) conscious

used to make Freud slap
his forehead or the desk,
grimace and insist "the brain
is not a topography in which
one consciousness is subterranean!"
But that was much later.
If the brain is not a map

it is even less a cooking utensil
and a skull with holes would mean
death at birth, not wise rule.
Colanderi's own theory was more supple,
an example of the deductions
that qualify him as one
of science's greatest detectives.

Colanderi met the King at a masquerade
where the latter was a mummy,
Egyptology having just become
all the rage in high society.
Otis was swaddled entirely, except
for one arm which he had left out
to hold a drink, wave to the public

and swing his partner in a polonaise
(or shuffle her, since his feet were bound
and Deirdre, as Nefertiti, wore
a headdress more hugely elaborate
than the cornucopias then in fashion
which forced millions of charm school girls
to walk with dictionaries on their heads).

As a dancing bear, Colanderi
had reduced peripheral vision
through the eyeholes of his costume
but his work in Spain had cued him
to the symptoms, so when Otis
lifted Deirdre's hand to signal
the start of the dance, and the other men

lifted their ladies' hands
to the violins' first chord,
then Otis refused to budge,
would not move the bare arm,
only Colanderi did not laugh; even Deirdre
thought the King witty, credited him
with a shaggy dog or mummy joke and laughed.

With the violins still on the chord
and the hundreds of paired hands
held aloft sweating, everyone
delighted to be present at the event
where the dance *glacier* was invented
(similar to the children's game of freeze),
only Colanderi was grim and watchful.

Deirdre's laugh toppled her hat
which made a zippy arc
in exactly the right place
to the left of Otis' face, breaking
the trance, and Colanderi knew:
the Dementia is optically triggered
and shall be optically cured.

Sure enough, the King's diapers were wet.
Since most of Colanderi's notebooks
were burned in the Fuchsia Siege
("undot my *i*," he is said
to have quipped, as the last book
was set aflame at his beheading),
we can only speculate

about how a stranger to our nation
coaxed the fact of the diaper
from the proud Queen, who presumably
became his mistress for several decades.
Lucy H. was imported from Spain.
(Stunning Lucy, played by Garbo
in the obscure 1919 film which may be

her most luminous performance,
has also been romantically linked
to the Queen, although not,
of course, in the Hollywood version.)
Colanderi could soon induce and end
a trance through swift
peripheral movement, a precursor

of the mesmerism technique
so popular in Dickens' day.
But the interesting question
of what in Otis and Lucy's eyeballs
got their attention so focused ahead
on the visually small, like cats
with catnip—the *why* of the trance—

Colanderi could not answer.
He was haunted by the failure
and held himself responsible
since undaunted research had increased
the incidence of trances to the point
where he could no longer tell
the real from the induced

(cf. Heisenberg's early notes
on the Uncertainty Principle
and Yeats on dancer vs. dance—
both men spent months entranced
by what is left of Colanderi's work).
Furthermore, Colanderi's own spells
had increased to the point

that he watched Otis as intently
as Otis watched the rose or mouse;
Deirdre watched husband and lover
(lovers, if we count Lucy)
lost in thought in the lab
reached through a secret portal
between torture chamber and wine cellar.

Once she waved a hand
in Otis' face, in crude imitation
of Colanderi's technique,
and broke three trances
in domino effect, returning the trio
to an animated discussion of fencing,
but more often than not

she was alone
with the heads of state
and her thoughts, which often turned
to the age-old brain-teaser:
did Colanderi study Dementia
because he was afflicted,
as madmen become psychiatrists

and violent men become policemen;
or did the study cause the affliction,
because a face made long enough
will stick? If the latter,
why was Deirdre herself not infected?
The answer, we now know—
or know for now—is genetic:

Dementia C. is carried
by X chromosomes,
making the odds half a dozen of one
or the other that it will hit
male children, which explains
why, ten childbirths and ten girls
later, no offspring

of the King and Queen suffered;
Lucy H. is an anomaly here,
like ten girls in a row, proving
that all odds are made to be beat.
Colanderi's optical insight
became more and more baroque
until leeches first soaked

in apothecary substances
were harnessed to treat liver,
lung and heart as well as brain—
experiments that, not surprisingly,
left all the subjects worse for wear.
Leeches, as Freud reminds us
in *The Question of Lay Analysis*,

were "a hypothesis like so many others
in the sciences; the very earliest ones
have always been rather rough,"
but Freud was wrong.
The early ones are always most ornate.
Only modernism has taught us
the cost of simplicity,

and just as "the little black dress"
is a tricky concept of fanciness—
the streamlining that elevates
Anna Karenina above her sister
in adultery and suicide, Emma Bovary—
science tends to go for broke.
Frankenstein's workshop

is the design equivalent
of Deirdre's Nefertiti hat; compared
to *that,* Colanderi's last theory
was Jackie's pillbox.
He had invented a needle
to pluck Dementia
from the eyeball like a splinter.

Deirdre refused. Battle ensued
over whether Otis and Lucy, still
in the dark about their conditions
(as was Colanderi himself),
should be made to see the light
so they could give informed consent.
That Colanderi imagined his subjects

would cheerfully risk being blinded
is testament to his failing insight,
but the gambler who loses everything
then finds a last dusty dime
in his pocket lining
will not use the coin
to open a savings account;

he must believe
the last shot will hit the jackpot,
and Colanderi would not be dissuaded
from the final operation.
Ironically, his "needle" was close
to the one ophthamologists now use
to peel the tiny "cloud"

on the cornea that causes
Dementia C.—more and more rarely,
as the growth is unlikely to develop
when myopia is corrected early.
Rainer Colanderi was on the money.
For those without a sixth sense
to whom seeing is believing,

eyeball-stabbing seems too radical
a cure for sporadic inattention,
yet Colanderi's needle was nothing
compared to the cures for madness
in use for centuries after his death—
shock treatment, or the lobotomies
for which Portuguese neuropsychiatrist

Antonio de Egas Moniz
won a Nobel Prize in 1949,
though he hadn't operated on a soul
since 1944, when a lobotomized patient
lodged a bullet in his spine,
rendering him a hemiplegic
(it is popularly held

that the lobotomized roll their heads
and tongues, forever stupid
in their chairs, but the worse travesty
is that after three months,
despite destroying over a hundred
square inches of brain matter,
the procedure leaves most patients

as violent as they were before).
One should not detest Moniz.
Chemotherapy too is brutal, yet
it often works—violent illnesses
beget violent cures; "an eye
for an eye," Colanderi joked.
In the movie, Deirdre awakens

in her sexy negligee
from a prophetic dream and hastens,
with a single candle, to the lab,
where she first sees gagged Lucy
strapped squirming in *her* nightie
to the damp wall, eyes bulging
(Colanderi would have put her

in a trance, not in bondage);
the camera then pans the shadow
of Colanderi's arm wielding the needle,
here more like an icepick
than the three-inch tool
in the British Museum, now believed
to be his final model;

Deirdre screams, the scream awakens Otis
and Otis, much as he hates to hurt
his friend, has him beheaded.
The narrative trick of "the nick
of time"—the wrist of the hand
with the knife grabbed mid-air,
the evil wedding stopped

not on *forever hold your peace*
but on *I now pronounce you man*—
is, of course, not realistic;
in life most things are erosions,
not earthquakes, most changes
not even slow but undetectable
until much later,

when hindsight makes an epiphany
of one note in the symphony.
For most of us, life itself
is a shaggy dog joke
with a disappointing punchline.
Colanderi's fate was more dramatic
not just because he was beheaded

but because life in the public eye
transforms the sow's ear of the daily
to the silk purse of art:
while most of our wedding pictures
are stilted, out of focus,
the bride's eyes red
as a rat's from the flash,

the weddings of the famous
are delicate and powerful at once,
gossamer and thunder, because
the famous are seasoned performers.
John F. Kennedy filmed not only
his wedding but his courtship
with socialite Jackie,

and in their home movies
on the sailboat, even their hair
in their eyes makes a statement—
Look at us. Our lives
are harmony, not random noise.
One may be nostalgic for the days
when experience was more direct,

when one had to read the book,
not wait for the movie or better
yet, be there in the flesh,
for those who missed the beheading
could not catch it later on the news.
But in fact there were merely
portrait painters and rumors,

not photographers and reporters;
it was even simpler to touch up
a story when staff
who strayed into the basement
were executed at royal discretion
and when news traveled slowly enough
to revise any story several times.

Thus we don't know exactly
how Deirdre engineered the Fuchsia Plot
that got her husband seeing red
against the incriminated Colanderi,
but we do know the official version
bespoke political treachery.
We also know there was no scene

at midnight in transparent nightgowns.
Not only was Lucy not strapped
to the wall; she had left
the country with a stable boy—
a story so popular in the court
where downward mobility was rare
that it almost overshadowed

the Fuchsia Siege itself.
If it weren't for Lucy's diary
which (in later legend)
was part of the booty robbed
by highwaymen who stowed away
on a ship to the Indies that sank,
the brocade book lodged

in a waterproof crevice
to be dredged up in our time
by a deep-sea diver whose sale
of the diary funded a heart
transplant for his young wife,
we would know even less
about Dementia Colander.

Deirdre's diary was worthless
by this point; leagues of scholars
have been unable to decipher as code
such terse, uninspired lines as
Fool funny today. Boar overcooked.
Even with Lucy's diary
and "A Pitiful Affliction of Kings"

(smuggled out by the activists
who assassinated Joel the Good),
our understanding of the research
is piecemeal as reconstructing
the skeletons of dinosaurs,
but we do know Colanderi
never got to try his needle.

We know that Lucy and the stableboy
led long and happy lives
in America, where none of their children
suffered from Dementia C.:
one daughter married a senator
and a son was instrumental
in the invention of the bicycle.

Interestingly, a great-granddaughter
did her own research and opined
that the disease was respiratory,
the result of corsets;
since most victims remained men
she was wrong, but we can hardly fault
her suffragette leaning.

As for Deirdre, she was never the same.
At thirty she suffered less
from eleven childbirths than from guilt
for betraying her lover, even if
so doing saved her husband's sight;
since she started the Fuchsia Siege
and the Fuchsia Siege started

the redivision of Europe
that led to ages of war,
she was also guilty of destroying
the continent's peace—that blink
of stillness like a spell of Dementia C.
in the days of history.
Otis died in his sleep.

All versions agree that the Queen
did not sleep or eat for sixty days,
during which she kept removing the gold coins
from the King's eyes and waving items
in his face, convinced
that any moment,
he would wake up.

Two

Happiness

What it is
is the absence of pain. Nothing more.

Over a decade of life in the bull's eye
of troubled cities in the Northeastern corridor

and I've never been raped,
never stabbed, burglarized, or even mugged

though I hate to say or even think
I never get colds

or hear a sportscaster brag
about a basketball player's percentage from the line

before the foul shot that would win the game:
why wave a red flag in the bull's face

if the bull is God
in happy pastures, chewing the grass?

Infinite disasters and fender-benders lurk
around each corner

like the black holes that claim stray socks
at the laundromat.

Best to notice happiness peripherally,
the way walking in a city

you take in a pretty weed
growing from a sidewalk crack

or a woman with slim ankles
passing briskly—to meet someone for a drink

perhaps, a man she has not seen,
back whole from a treasure hunt or war.

You, too, have someone waiting at home
and for a goosebumped second you know

that you are loved. That nothing,
at least today, has gone wrong.

A Goldfish in a Bag

Grasshoppers were worse.
Even battering themselves
against the glass,
they barely knew the difference
between inside and outside the jar.

You let them go not from mercy,
but from boredom.
The goldfish couldn't go.
A bag of water was a better fate
for it than the continent

or the continent's whole
capsized bowl of sky.
All that kept your fish from death
were your hands—
huge for the first time—

and a sandwich bag
you saw through to organs
pale as a blister under iodine.
The fish, one eye at a time,
observed the hands

its life was in and shivered
as you did when you stayed
in the pool too long.
Soon it would float belly-up
in a glass, lifeless as dentures.

Bat and Skyscraper

A mound of money
which a baseball bat
would get lost in like a needle
in your kitchen when you stagger
for coffee, with a note
like a Christmas tree star at the top

exhorting you to rejoice
because the authorities
are lightyears from suspecting
would be more useful
if not more surprising
than a dead bat in mid-town—

at the foot of the granite high rise,
how very tiny!
And like the squirrel, how clever
a mutation on the standard rodent!
Though geese are at home
strung up near a basket of fruit,

bats don't die
but rather fly across the moon
forever, in distress, caught
in the act of being hideous.
You'd blacken "dead bat"
on a multiple-choice test

to indicate what item's out of place
in a city, like a baked Alaska
orphaned in a family
of hat, shoe, cumberbund;
or the alligator from the sewer
which appeared in your bathroom

the morning you were dressing
for your wedding—
on its hind legs, not carnivorous
but blinking, lost,
wanting, like a kitten,
a dish of milk.

Lesson

The caveman, dead 100,000 years,
has been revivified on the brink
of the twenty-first century.
Take a blink to accept this as a premise
so we can get on with business:
the scientist, having exchanged names
with his Neanderthal friend
and shared dinner
(spaghetti, dungbettles, whatever)
around the lab's lifelike campfire,
feels he should explain
that tricky concept, *year*.

Outside, the scientist points to the moon.
The caveman nods or grunts
to indicate comprehension.
Now the scientist enacts a luau mime
of breasts and a shapely walk.
The caveman shrugs or squints: in his day
women evidently did not act
like *femmes fatales* from a Hitchcock film.
A brave female colleague is dug up
so the caveman can touch or sniff if looking
won't do it, sex obfuscated by the labcoat.
So far, so good.

Luckily, our man hails from a gentle tribe
and does not think the woman is a gift.
Now the scientist pricks his finger,
displays blood, points downward on the woman,
points back to the moon: eureka!
Ten of them, the scientist explains,
and you've got a baby (mime of tiny, wailing
creature); *twelve and you've got a year.*
The scientist counts off on his fingers,
but his pupil is lost. They round up
some objects—foodstuffs are deemed
easiest, apples or lab rabbits—

and place them on the table: *one*
(a cautionary finger raised), *two*
(Churchill's V) and so forth—
this takes a while as apples roll
off the table, rabbits dart;
the caveman is distracted by the objects
themselves, tries to use the pencil
the scientist takes notes with
to kill a rabbit—so by the time he understands
counting, it's too late to correlate
the principle with menstruation and the moon.
Tomorrow is, as they say, another day.

By sunlight they try again: sun, moon,
woman, food, footage of tides and crops.
Needless to say, there are distractions,
like the fellow's fascination
with the movie image, with the urinal
he is brought to in the morning,
the toothbrush, the scientist's shaven face
and the angry gestures of the lady anthropologist
who has been summoned to help and thinks
it disgraceful they are trying to impose
their culture on the man, rather than
letting him teach them of his own.

Though the man is quick and curious
and seems to have a calm space in his brain
for the miraculous, so that traffic
(they'd feared his reaction to automobiles)
delights him, at this rate it will take years
to explain *year,* and who knows
if he'll live long enough to acquire
the catalogue of images that make
the concept meaningful: the flipping pages
of the calendar, the hourglass, the punched
timeclock and happy bell when school lets out,
rings on trees and candles on birthday cakes.

They race against the clock
because journalists now have the scoop
and just as in the movies are plaguing
the laboratory doors, so that to take
the caveman to the beach, forest, or zoo,
to a department store or airport
he must be smuggled out a back door
like a politician or rock star.
He knows who his friends are and hides
from the camera's flash like Dracula
(a crucifix, however, does nothing for him).
They are hopeful. Look at Helen Keller.

The caveman's a good sport, a fast learner.
"I remember," the relaxing scientist
tells the anthropologist (they're lovers
now, bound by joint concern for their charge)
"how in college I wished
I were back in grade school knowing
what I knew by then—
how smart I would have seemed!
I wonder if that's how he feels."
Across the room, the caveman examines
the dirt under his nails and yawns,
like anyone biding time.

Dying in Your Dreams

I did not care
for the pale green, maybe Biedermeier bowl
at the auction, would not have even bid
unless you insisted, no less
died for it. How stupid!
You were stabbed too
but as the depth of field narrowed I lost you
to the pain
and the phone booth I crawled towards,
a vanishing point past millions of buildings.
My death was slow and frantic
like rush hour traffic.

Right before bed I had bounded the steps
from the loft, hit my head
on the ceiling and bawled.
I haven't cried like that since I was ten!
When your wisdom tooth was pulled,
you said when I was calm, you wept
though there was no pain,
no sensation even through the Novacaine;
there must simply be a connection
between nerve and tear duct,
as some claim a bond
between nightmare and full bladder.

True, after I screamed and woke you
we took turns in the bathroom,
but the way pain irradiated from that wound
was too deep for a mere alarm
of imminent incontinence, so real I must
know more about death than I think.
If there's a death wish it's the wish
to know—and live to tell the tale.
How you'll die, and when, and how it feels.
But they say you never die in dreams.
Dead, you later theorized,
there's not much to do.

As if it were a matter of plot
and pacing, the protagonist
not getting shot in the opening credits,
Hamlet not killing the King
right away, so you have a play.
Maybe. But maybe your own death
is simply too brutal to witness,
like your own conception
with your parents' door flung wide
because you were supposed to be asleep.
I had a bad dream!
It's better as an adult.

I scream, wake you.
And though moist women may have been
seducing you among mangoes,
bright-beaked birds and sunken galleons
to which you do not fall or sink
but float, you manage to say
There, there and provide
a here in which I am
in perfect health, yards from a bathroom.
Still, there is that slice of life
alone at dawn, so far from a phone,
when you believe you never will wake up.

The bathroom light so strange
you might have wakened naked
in the future, unaware of cars, or phones,
or what war's being fought.
What if death is just like this?
Not even sure if you're awake or not
you scream, and pee, then
like the concussion victim
are afraid to return to sleep
because you know your death waits there,
in place where it left off, unreal enough
for you to assume you're dreaming.

The Mesopotamian Tool Room

A man with an ancient cigar
and a barking, three-legged dog
fixed dismembered cars
in the old neighborhood for years
with tools just like the tools
you are assigned to guard.
The Mesopotamian wing is in the basement,
dark as a torture chamber,
and except for the weekend father
who marches progeny through
a microwave tour of man's progress,
no one comes here by design.

Teenagers in search of a place to neck
think it avant garde to suggest
a quickie on the floor with history
as the voyeur, but they never follow through.
Any single man here is a rapist;
any woman is ripe and curvaceous
against the decay of Mesopotamia.
You invent a plot for them—
the hunchback of Notre Dame
and Botticelli's Venus meet, turn out
to be cousins, marry anyway—
but this takes, what? Ten seconds?

And you've got decades of timeclocks to punch
before you can retire
to tell your grandchildren what?
Mesopotamia invented the toothbrush?
They don't even need a guard here.
People slash the Mona Lisa's smile
and giddy-up the brontosaurus skeleton,
but no one since Mesopotamia
has craved a Mesopotamian buttonhook.
You'd love to catch an archaeologist
with his hand in the cookie jar
or better yet, leave out

milk and cookies for him,
let him take everything,
Santa Claus with the film in reverse
to the beginning of time,
before Mesopotamia, when cockroaches
were the latest model, the first
crustaceans to learn to walk.
Almost asleep in your chair,
you see lights flicker and swear
the tools themselves are trying to escape,
grieved in their display case
like live lobsters in a tank.

Woman, 78, Caught Shoplifting

John always warned me
I'd be one of those old ladies
in an upstairs window
who boils water to toss on the dog
squatting in the scrawny tulips.
John took vitamins and stayed fit,
tempting fate to cheap irony,
whereas I was prepared
from infancy to fight Death off
with my pocketbook.

Just as cheap women marry jobless men
and jealous men marry flirts,
a meek man like John was bound
to find a misanthrope.
He was not as sweet as he seemed
nor I as sour, but if marriage
sands some edges, it roughens others,
and my role with John was doomsayer.
If I had an inch of hair
for each hour I've sat by the window

petitioning against injustice below,
my braid would be long enough
for John to grab from the grave.
I stole him a wallet.
That dead he doesn't need it
is irrelevant: no shoplifter, except
maybe in Turkey, steals groceries.
It's not getting something for nothing
(though that helps, in this economy)
so much as putting something in something:

like children who stick everything
that glitters in their mouths, we want
a world that's small and fits.
Perhaps we weren't breastfed right.
Perhaps, as the Mayor suggested
on television (not that he budgeted
to solve the problem),
people who have paid taxes
since the stock market crashed
will not feel less abandoned

licking cake bowls, weaving potholders.
Though we shrink, we are not
helpless as children
lost in department stores
with mittens pinned to their coats.
We vote. We remember an address
and can board, slowly, a bus.
If we deal with grief and arthritis
we can surely bear the eyes
of badly disguised store detectives

skimming us before alighting
on the gangster teens whom we disgust,
despite the fact that we are like them,
our bodies strange even to us.
In Science Class we, too, hunched three
to a microscope for the peep show
of hydra dividing and merging,
our bodies the watched pots
that refused to boil, then curdled—
only witchcraft resolved the image

between voices bass or soprano,
acne dormant or volcanic.
The teenagers steal jewelry, clothing.
They may even enjoy the thought
of detectives with hidden cameras
watching them undress. Who would watch us?
Still, the old rarely take clothes.
I've lifted a pair of black men's socks,
soft to the touch; a plain,
old-fashioned corkscrew; the wallet,

also black, with compartments
for cash, credit cards and photographs
of loved ones to show the men at work.
Such objects slide easily
from our palms to the pockets
of the coats we wear, even in summer.
At home these items go in the top drawer
of John's bureau, which is just
as he left it, just as my father's was
and maybe every man's: expired license,

loose coins, letters from old lovers.
I haven't read these—even the dead
deserve some privacy.
Had I not been caught
I would have transferred John's license
and bills, the business cards of people
he would never have called, from the old
wallet to the new—a ritual, the way women
after heartbreak often get haircuts
to demarcate a fresh start.

Occasionally I might have removed a bill,
for the Sunday paper or a child
selling candy bars door to door—
John had come from the bank the day
he died, and the crisp new bills he got
are still as good as any—and felt
exactly as I would have if he were home.
The smell of the leather reminds me
of department stores and thus of John,
because to me his brain

was always like the huge stores
that occupied my childhood Saturdays.
No heaven could have been more crammed
with bright, warm things to want,
but it was easy to get lost
and hard to find the bathroom;
in the ladies' lounge, old women rocked,
knitted, or talked to themselves,
so when you entered, all their faces
turned at once—it was terrifying.

Other times I imagine his brain
as the console air controllers use
to plot the route of planes: millions
of computer lines shooting everywhere,
more complex than a map but geometrical,
crisper, like how the plan of this store
must have looked to the architect
before the tangle of objects
destroyed the symmetry.
So I browse, thinking of John, as if

by touching leather or silk I travel
a hand down his muscle or bone, and when
I reach for what I finally take
some merge takes place—just the familiar,
like knowing what he'd say before
he said it or how tying the trash bag
was my job, taking the trash out his.
This time, a hand on my wrist:
the store detective, embarrassed.
They escorted me to a room upstairs

where, on many monitors, you could watch
the shoppers pick up objects,
put them down, pick them up again—
fascinating what a violation
it seemed, as if we penetrated
secret places in their thoughts.
They made me empty my pockets.
No strip search, of course, but they felt
the keys which I wear, like many old women
forced to take public transportation

along with the city's more unsavory
characters, on a belt under my clothes,
separate from my identification, so
if my handbag is wrenched from me
the thief will not know where I live.
They scolded me. Reported how much
the store loses from such activity
(my heart did not bleed), told me
the consumer pays (don't we anyway?),
then told me some stories.

Once a woman in a mink tried to liberate
a puppy from the Pet Department as an act
of mercy. Before he worked here,
one of the detectives cased a grocery store,
where a streetperson might steal
a pound of ground chuck to eat raw,
with his hands—the detectives never prosecuted,
any more than they'd prosecute me.
They took the wallet back
and were stern;

they hoped I'd be humiliated
to have my daughter fetch me.
Maybe they even thought I wanted,
like a failed suicide, to be caught,
wanted attention from them and my neglectful
daughter, but in fact she is very sweet.
So is my grandson. Everyone agrees
he's the spitting image of John,
but the older he gets, the less
I see the resemblance.

Saturday Morning Cartoons

Pig, dog, cat, mouse, duck
identically rasped, huffed
and chortled like our parents'
friends who smoked too much.
We let our parents sleep.
The violence of cartoons
we knew even then was not
escapism but verisimilitude.
Like adults the animals
defended territory
and time, tried to carve
a moment's crevice
in the suburbs
between ghetto and wilderness
but always rebounded from
the oven of work
to the frying pan of home
with its leak, dead battery
and filthy laundry piled
so high the ants
attracted by our crumbs
built a school, a factory
to sap the spirit
of the father ant
and never could be teargassed
out with us always
underfoot—couldn't we
go somewhere and play
quietly or watch TV?
So we did. I personally
had no intention of ever
living like that.
We sat, cheered
by the thought that some
other kid's father
had to sit alone

67

in a dark little room
cranking out cartoons
for our amusement
before breakfast, a frame
for each movement.

Gypsy Moths

Some friends can't understand
how I can be close to my parents
when my father beat me
and my mother stood by, letting it happen
or intervened out of fear for him, not me
("Stop it, Joe—you're going
to have a heart attack").

Of course Dot and Joe insisted
back when I beat on the topic, when they
(as they liked to point out) were paying
for psychotherapy as well as tuition,
that *beat* was wanton hyperbole
and even then I was inclined
to believe them, not only

because victims often take the blame
(raped women "have it coming")
but because even now I am
an unreliable witness who woefully
exaggerates, all statistics trumped.
Still, it is a fact that I left
for summer camp one year—the year

that my bunkmates planted under my pillow
a bullfrog, which was supposed
to leap out, but it suffocated—
with a black eye.
My brother and sister both remember hiding
under tables in tears
while I was knocked about,

and if I was a "difficult child,"
the obvious question is why.
Why, at nine years old, did I suffer
from psychosomatic blindnesses
during Math class that forced me
to be led to the school nurse
then dragged every Saturday morning

to a child psychiatrist near the zoo?
After these sessions, my father always
took me to a Hot Shoppe for hash browns.
The diagnosis: classical Electra Complex.
Hard to argue when my stories at the time
were about a bird family
in which the mother bird fell from the nest

but the father and daughter bird
(no siblings in the sublimated version)
got on fine without her.
A later psychiatrist suggested
that maybe I just didn't like Math.
She believed that my harangues
against my violent father were a smokescreen

for the real problem: Mom.
How could I think my mother loved me
when I knew, from the Bill Lucy incident
(Bill had taken to tormenting me at school
and when he finally ripped my dress
down the back with a pocket knife
while I was bent over a water fountain

my mother marched to his house,
grabbed him by the collar, and threatened
murder if he ever touched me again),
my mother's power, yet she would not
wield it for me against my father?
In a quaint restaurant with a lover
in Perugia, Italy, in 1985, decades after

my parents were anything but charming,
I could still cry discussing this,
as if motherlove were a wash of sunlight
and I the frail, stunted houseplant.
If the Freudians are right, then everything
can be traced to that primal neglect.
"You can feel that," my companion said,

"but in your more grown-up head
you must realize it's not so simple;
if you were your child, you'd beat you too."
As we know from concentration camp inmates
stealing a homeland from the Palestinians
and affirmative action decisions
making it sticky for white males

with seniority, two rights can often
make a wrong. It could have been worse:
I was always fed, never molested;
I was not raised in an orphanage
by angry nuns with rulers; while my father
had been known to hurl
a plate of spaghetti at my head

when I spilled a drink,
he also took me to museums and zoos
and was proud of me, in some sense;
while some psychologists insist
a random reinforcement of praise and blame
is a worse fate for a child, the people
I most like now all had trying childhoods.

The fundamental tenet of psychoanalysis,
so Judeo-Christian: suffering strengthens.
My mother's father died when she was two
and she was abandoned to an old granny
so her mother could pursue a new man;
when Dot was reclaimed, she already had
a stepbrother, much preferred.

Her shoes never fit, thus her misshapen feet.
My father slept four to a bedbuggy mattress—
head, foot, head, foot, often a toe
in his nose—with four siblings,
the oldest of whom, Harry,
was institutionalized for schizophrenia
after he ran naked in winter across

the Brooklyn Bridge reciting Communist verse;
every Sunday for almost forty years
a sibling has visited him in the loony bin.
To us, Harry is nothing more
than a threatening, slightly cross-eyed
ancestor in the scrapbook
we've looked at so often

we know the pictures by heart:
my mother at fourteen, the buttons of her blouse
pulled slightly apart (how badly
she wanted a bra and her freckles gone);
us as infants, bland and blond,
anonymous, yet some tension in our posture
prefiguring future personality

as my father's swagger in the sailor uniform
suggests his sneaky wit tonight,
at this family gathering.
Aunt Ruth is complaining about children
who write spiteful autobiographies
biting the hands of celebrities
who fed them—the ingrates!

Don't you believe, my brother asks,
that Joan Crawford beat her daughter?
No, Ruth says, and even if it's true
how disgusting to tell the world so.
Baiting his sister, Dad asks who Ruth thinks
has the power, the parent or the child?
"The parent always does," he says,

"for years and years, so if the child finally
strikes back, who's to blame?"
Ruth retorts with statistics
on child molestation—she thinks
all that's invented to spite the parents.
We smile at each other: no way
to win an argument with Ruth.

Strange how rarely I argue with my parents.
They are witty, generous, their refrigerator
stuffed to the gills with delicacies
(I'd always assumed they stocked
for our visits, but my brother remarked
that a five-pound jar of ketchup
indicates otherwise).

"You need to put on some weight,"
my mother always says, as mothers will,
with her cool hand on my cheek or arm:
"How lovely to see you." My father,
cigar in mouth, asks us to join him
on "the grounds"—a wry description
of his suburban quarter-acre,

though we children cannot match
our parents' standard of living
in food stock or real estate,
our dwellings never as clean or inviting;
even our television reception is poorer.
Outside, my father frets about gypsy moths.
They are devouring his huge pin oaks.

The oaks wear skirts, and he has sprayed
the leaves as high as he could reach,
but the insects are plentiful and hardy.
We watch one caterpillar (they are not
moths yet, their whole cycle just
ten days—"they eat, lay eggs, and die,"
my father says, shaking his head,

"what a life")—crawl painstakingly
around the burlap skirt to find the bark.
All along the house's aluminum siding,
caterpillars make their obstinate ascent.
My father is killing them one by one
with the tip of the key to his Japanese car.
"I don't think that's going to do it,"

my sister observes, but Dad, coughing
from the cigar, says every bit helps.
Later that night, after a glut of movies
on the VCR (nothing at our house
in moderation), he brings us outside.
The gypsy moths are munching in the dark:
an otherworldly racket, like the crunch

of breakfast cereals in commercials.
You can hear the insects' excrement
hitting the pavement in the driveway,
a chorus of delicate pellets.
"By the morning," my father says sadly,
"the whole driveway will be covered
with shit, the leaves shot full of holes;

in three days the leaves will be gone."
The exterminator is supposed to come
tomorrow, but the forecast predicts rain
to wash away the spray. "How did the trees
get to be this old?" he asks.
"How did they survive this long?"
My mother smiles: "your father,"

she confides, "must always have something
to worry about." Remarkable how much
she loves him, for how long:
we can't touch such devotion
with our own mates, at least not yet.
We had always assumed my father
would die first; now we're not so sure.

My mother has complained
about a pain in her chest.
She falls asleep on the couch, TV on,
as if she doesn't deserve the luxury
of bed and darkness,
as during family dinners
she eats standing up while serving us.

We tiptoe past to the upstairs room
with the scrapbooks where, at 3 AM,
we huddle by a window to watch
our lone father
like a mad scientist or Martian
on the lawn in the dark with a flashlight,
still going at caterpillars with his key.

Decisions, Decisions

You are eating something, or just sitting there,
when the call comes: "Are you happy?"
They offer to pay you more
to do a job like what you do now, only better,
with different people, in a different city.
You are flattered, and consider.

Maybe the new job is fated: consider
how you were just sitting there
when the call came, hating your dull, cold city.
There's nothing to do there. You'd be happy
to go somewhere new and lively with better
people, art, shops, and restaurants, more

money and opportunity, more
of what a city's for. You consider
whether your city will ever get better.
Not when all the good people hightail out of there
for the Sunbelt, San Francisco, Seattle—happy
places. Every city is Emerald City

compared to your blighted nightmare of a city.
You've lived here so long you hardly notice anymore.
You've grown complacent—not happy
but in stabilized decay, like the city. Consider
this, however: how do you know it will be better there?
After all the trouble you could discover you were better

off where you were. Would it be better
psychologically to make a change, even if the new city
is as bad or worse, even if there
are factors which make the job more
trouble than it's worth? So much to consider!
Contemplating change puts a strain even on a happy

person, which you're not. You're happy
only when you soothe yourself that things will get better
someday. But what if it's foolish to consider
that life comes down to a better job or a better city?
You try to tell yourself that anywhere is only more
of the same, that this is all there

is: a person waiting to be happy in a dead city.
But you can't believe that *nothing* will get better anymore.
You have to at least consider getting out of there.

Needlepoint Guernica

A block from Notre Dame
which is, a sign reminds, a shrine
to "the cult of Catholicism"
and not a museum,
two filthy children flanked us
and stagily kissed our wrists.
We couldn't brush or shove them off.
Along the Seine with its smell
of urine, antique and fresh,
contradicting the glitter
of sandblasted buildings,

men who sell "originals"
of monuments—always head-on
in full sun, as if Impressionism
never happened—must have watched us
slap two gypsy children
in tatters hyperbolic as German
Expressionist urchin costumes
(the dirt, however,
was not theatrical make-up).
What made you reach for your wallet
the moment I swooped

for the boy's neck?
You claim I saw subliminally,
as you did, the quick arc of his hand
from you to his jacket,
then was jarred by them stepping back
after so much relentlessness.
Two bystanders sent up a cry
of thief and struck the boy I still
held by the neck, who gave
the wallet back and cried,
or was that only after

someone cried police?
Humiliating to fog up such an easy
sequence, our bumbling
in contrast to their control.
In dance, comedy, crime, and self-defense,
timing is what separates
the artist from the dabbler.
Your money, passport still intact,
you grumbled let them go,
disgusting grubs.
Two blocks and six stories later

we ran the tap at once,
giving new dimension to the phrase
"to wash your hands of it," then realized
the men we'd thanked were coaches,
there to pass the wallets to
and institute Plans A, B, or C
depending on degree of danger,
our version entailing stage punches
and diversionary indignation.
For no reason but adrenalin
we returned to the scene of the crime

to find, of course, pickpockets gone.
The difference between life and art:
life is harder to revise
for moral clarity.
Were the men good citizens or accomplices?
What was worse, to thus corrupt a child
or for a child to be that corrupt
all on his own?
And the girl-child was so beautiful.
A close-up of her baleful eyes
would make a fine accusatory ad

for charity—why indeed
hadn't we agreed to free them
if they would pose for a snapshot
with the men who helped us,
all of us mugging
like a champion little league team?
Already we had what the French
call *esprit de l'escalier,*
when you turn at the bottom
of the stairs to say
what you should have said at the top.

We let the urchins hover,
gargoyle-like, over dinner,
but after dinner we craved old photographs
of Paris to flesh out the city
which exists in the brain,
elusive as the aftertaste
of cheese at that edge of readiness
that's blinding, not overexposed.
The stillness of old photographs
would make us feel less like tourists
than like astronauts uncovering Atlantis.

Instead, in a shop about to close,
we found an Auschwitz picture book.
I never want to look and always do.
Was that the worst crime in history?
You thought the French Revolution
would photograph as poorly.
That Nazis documented the atrocity,
I said, was precisely what made them
worst, but you thought
there would be home movies
of the Crucifixion, had Romans film.

Nazis were merely the first
to mix primitive with high tech—
the witch in the gingerbread house
plotting children's deaths
with computers and a large, efficient staff.
Outside the sky was skeined
with one of those Paris dusks
that imprints on the retina
because its colors risk
being too intense, too much
like an aerial postcard of Paris

rather than the Paris you walk through
and always risk forgetting:
grain and shadow, mutations
of gray and beige more infinite
than the gallons of blood
washed from cobblestone
in the city's history.
How could we hope
to sort out pickpockets
or Holocaust, our biggest problem
whether to eat rare duck or veal?

How calmly the Auschwitz inmates posed;
some even smiled, with barbed wire
rather than Eiffel Tower as background,
as if the wish for happiness
(or at least equilibrium)
were so great that amidst
the worst earthquake, someone
would improvise a picnic, play the flute.
I should be fed to the lions
as punishment for making such a fuss
over where I'm seated at restaurants.

What if, I asked, the impulse to art
were nothing more than a vanity
to document our time on earth,
like buffalo on cave walls
or my best friend's mother
in Silver Spring, Maryland,
who at age sixteen
carved *I was here* in Polish
in the wood of her bed at Bergen-Belsen
with a rusty nail—
in the bunk above her, Anne Frank slept.

A flu killed Anne Frank
but not my neighbor,
who ten years later
bought The World Book and orthodonture
for her daughter's posterity
despite the lesson of history.
You said: that's not art.
Heart-wrenching as we find
such death-camp graffiti,
art in general needs
leisure, contemplation.

No one having his bones crushed
one by one dwells on a sunset,
the luscious curve
of a dancer's instep;
no one blindfolded for the firing squad
can concentrate on pain
enough to make pain vivid
to someone in an easy chair.
Political art hasn't time
for innovation; the starving
don't age cheese or wine.

Anne Frank, I agreed, did not keep
her diary in the camp.
The question of whether the diary
is naive art or artistic documentary
is moot because it moves us
and is an original by a girl
precocious even for the privileged class
who would not live to undercut
her hope and openness
with the pessimism and mistrust
that marked us all, after the war—

And we do love a dead artist,
especially one who dies poor
and is not too prolific.
What if Anne had kept a diary
until her death at eighty in Silver Spring?
What if eighty such diaries were found,
common as the arrowheads and vases
we walk by in museums? Worse yet,
what if the diary were written
by a girl born in Silver Spring, Maryland,
the war invented?

"Miss Frank has a gift
for the language, but has not yet found
her subject." It's true,
you said (or at least I think you did;
by this point we were lost
in Paris and our talk,
the Seine crossed more than once
as we stopped to examine a cornice molding
or the interesting shoes
of a woman with a Dachshund):
art's rare, suffering wholesale.

Did "Guernica" make me think
of Spain, or of Picasso himself:
muscular arms crossed on an imposing chest,
bald head tan and unabashed?
The latter, I confessed.
That's what I like about you—
you have such an eye for human folly.
And cornice moldings, you added.
Your point was that Hitler
could not have written
a happy little travelogue

about a summer with his dog
unless the dog was rabid
in a picnic basket in the trunk.
On the contrary! Let Hitler write
his travelogue, I said;
let Anne Frank become a Hell's Angel
but later convert, a Jew for Jesus.
The more twists the merrier,
though I must confess the ironies
of experimental art
can also be tedious and sentimental:

a snapshot of a tourist
posing his family before the Louvre
is as dull as framing a shot
of your own loved ones, probably
duller to your survivors.
A traveler's clash:
I wanted honest snaps of us abroad
in love, before vistas of river
and rooftop, whereas you like
myopic, arty shots
of doorknobs or the texture

of spray paint on venerable walls.
At the Louvre you photographed the floors.
I like you better now that I know
how you use architectural detail
as melody for your baroque daydreams.
Your thought is formal and free-form
at once, like good sex,
speaking of which—
no, we were too full
of dinner and the intimidating
multiplicity of life on earth.

Besides, it was our last night.
Paris is a city you can miss
before you leave,
its beauty a post-coital ache
because you're disconnected
from both your life
and the artful concentration
that unleashes you from the daily.
Such floating moments
would make an art manifesto
if there weren't such a clash

between manifesto and the haze
of moments when consciousness
has not yet clicked into place:
before falling asleep,
when dreams are a taste
behind the teeth; or falling
out of love with someone
whose skin stretches differently
from the change in emotion—
the face not horrifying,
one eye here and one on the chin

as in "Guernica,"
but just *off,*
like your own face photographed.
An art that makes the moment
momentous is a tightrope:
if the border is written
in invisible ink between
pink and undercooked in chicken,
aroma and ammonia in a Brie,
then how much harder to get
a candid neither posed nor blurry.

By this point in our walk
the urchins had boiled down
to his hand in your pocket,
my hand on his neck—that one
parabola, symbolic as dance—
but the more we talked
about the incident isolated
from an oceanic week in Paris,
the more the freeze-frame
instantly replayed
reduced the experience

from emblemmatic to episodic,
until soon we said "you had
to be there"—a line
for tourists, not artists.
In fact many people *were* there.
Awaiting a late plane the next day,
we heard anecdotes of other tourists'
scuffles with children well-trained
to spot rich foreigners
who won't stay to press charges—
"not that you can prosecute

a minor, especially a minor
who is not a citizen," we'd say
enough times to hear our story
sadly common as a bad charter or
"Where were you when Kennedy was shot,"
but such sadness is a luxury.
Only the blessed
have their pockets picked
in Paris, France, then go on
to bemoan the Holocaust
after chevre and Bordeaux.

Vacations, like dreams, are found art:
you are ripped from days
alike as lined sheets
in a legal pad and fingerpainted
into a world where people have eaten,
slept, made love for years, without you.
A woman at dinner
looked past her companion
(as I did mine, to notice her)
at other couples silhouetted
at their tables

like the shoreline of an island
she had longed for in a magazine.
Undeniably, inexplicably French
in her glossy dress,
she was magical as finding,
at the beach,
a huge, whole conch.
The shell isn't art,
since its pleasure doesn't last
and can't be shared, but who cares?
Mona Lisa's smile is less ambiguous

than sailing to sleep
anchored by your arms
in a strange bed—
what an odd ship to be captain of
the brain is!
The spots before my eyes
that night became potatoes,
gnarled and raw—did you know,
I woke you up to say,
that potatoes only caught on in Europe
because they grew underground

and could have a war fought atop them
without causing a famine?
Uh-huh, you said, already transported
to your own battlefields.
How talented you are
to fight such wars and wake up
fresh-faced, in the right century.
War's for those
who can't afford to travel
was the next-to-last thing
I thought that night,

our last officially in Paris,
though for months we'd both
spend sleep there, wandering,
missing planes or catching them
at the last, most gorgeous
second, miraculous
as the pickpocket's speed-of-light hand
or Anne Frank on tiptoe
for years in the narrow house.
The last thing I thought:
art isn't everything.

The Brittingham Prize in Poetry

The University of Wisconsin Press Poetry Series

RONALD WALLACE, *General Editor*

Places/Everyone
JIM DANIELS

Talking to Strangers
PATRICIA DOBLER

Saving the Young Men of Vienna
DAVID KIRBY

Pocket Sundial
LISA ZEIDNER